ON EAGLES' WINGS

Getting where God wants you to be...on time

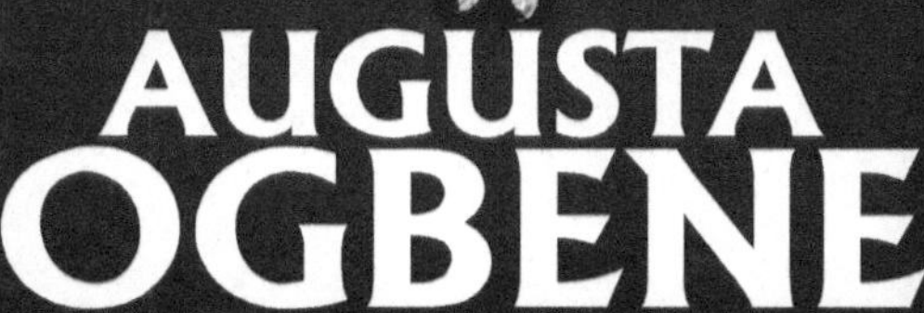

AUGUSTA OGBENE

ON EAGLES' WINGS

Dr Augusta Ogbene

Published by:
KINGS VIEW PUBLISHING HOUSE
41 Mayne Avenue, Calabar, Nigeria
www.kingsviewbooks.com
E-mail: enquiries@kingsviewbooks.com
+2348039263652; +234(0)7035358454

© Dr Augusta Ogbene 2019

ISBN: 978-978-55441-9-0

For information, please address:

DR AUGUSTA OGBENE
Christian Women Intercessors For All Nations
Asaba
Delta State
Nigeria
+2348036769278

Unless otherwise stated, all Scripture quotations are taken from the King James Version of the Holy Bible.

National Library of Nigeria Cataloguing in Publication Data
A catalogue record for this book is available from the Nigeria National Library.

Printed in the Federal Republic of Nigeria

 Dedication

To all my children and grandchildren who are emerging eagles in their generation.

Acknowledgments

I am deeply indebted to the Blessed Holy Spirit for the grace and revelation He provided for this work. Indeed, there's no level of education, intellect or human wisdom that can explain the deep things of God; only He can!

I specially appreciate my Rainbow Husband, Engineer Ehinomen Ogbene, for his encouragement and understanding during the times of keen attention given this work.

I equally appreciate all my children and grandchildren, my jewels of inestimable value, for always giving me reasons to rejoice in the work God has handed into my hands.

I appreciate every member of Christian Women intercessors for All Nations (CWIFAN) for all the selfless service in the Lord's Vineyard.

To my publisher, Brother Idongesit Okpombor, and the entire Kings View Publishing House team, I say a special "thank you."

May God bless you all in Jesus' Name. Amen!

Introduction

For many years now, I have read about the life of the eagle, listened to sermons on this wonderful bird, and also shared a bit on it. It is so wonderful to know how beautifully the Scripture compares God's tender care and workings in the life of His people to that of the eagle.

It is reported that the eagle is very affectionate to its young. It carefully nourishes its young. Being swift of flight and strong of wing, in a remarkable manner it takes its young upon it, and safely and swiftly conveys it where it pleases.

The eagle excels other birds both in its strength and in the size of its body. And especially, its pectoral muscles, by which its wings are supported, are very strong, so that it can carry its young and other things, on its back and wings.

Whereas other birds carry their young between their feet, for fear of those that fly above them, the eagle flying above all others, carries its young upon its wings to assist them in their flight.

It is said that the eagle, by flying high, is out of danger, and by carrying her birds on her wings rather than in her talons declares her love.

The story is told in ancient Babylon, of a lad

Dr. Augusta Ogbene

being thrown down from the top of a tower. An eagle, being a very quick sighted bird, saw him, flew under him, took him upon its back, and carried him into a garden, and gently let him down.

The story is also related of a man who was cast headlong into a deep ditch where they used to throw condemned malefactors. An eagle flew under him, and bore him on its wings, and carried him to the bottom, without any hurt to any part of his body.

These illustrations can make it a little clearer what God meant when He said He bore Israel on Eagles' wings. God means that He bestowed upon His people the same tender and powerful care of an eagle.

He bore them up mightily when they might have fallen. He supported their first flight as fledglings, and so saved them from disaster. He covered them, protected them, and

Dr. Augusta Ogbene

sustained them as the eagles' wings do its young.

Egypt was the nest in which Israel – God's young eaglets - were first formed as the embryo of a nation. When they increased in their numbers and grew to some level of maturity, they were carried out of that nest.

The Lord showed an affectionate concern for them, took them under His care and protection, stood between them and the Egyptians in a pillar of cloud, secured them from their arrows, and swiftly and safely removed them from the land of Egypt to the Promised Land.

Now, I think the most important part of what God did for Israel appears in the last line of Exodus 19:4, and is much more instructive. It conveys the whole essence or reason why God bore them on eagles' wings in the first place. Exodus 19:4 says, "*Ye have*

Dr. Augusta Ogbene

seen what I did unto the Egyptians, and how I bare you on eagles' wings, and brought you unto myself."

God brought them out of Egypt on Eagles' wings, that He might bring them UNTO HIMSELF. He brought them out of Egypt and its corrupting influences and led them back to His pure worship.

In other words, they were not only brought into a state of liberty, but into covenant and communion with God. This is what God aims at, in virtually everything He does, to bring us back to Himself, in whom alone we can be happy.

God explained to Moses that when He called him down to Egypt to lead His people out, He wanted Moses to understand that He was bringing them not to a land, but to a Person. So He said to them, "I brought you unto myself." This is what the Lord wants.

Dr. Augusta Ogbene

Think about it, after so many years of serving the Lord, the Apostle Paul said, "*My great goal in life is to know the Lord, to come unto Him.*"

Beloved, no matter what level you are in God, He still wants to bring you to Himself in a deeper experience of communion. It is my hope, therefore, that as you prayerfully read through this book, God will grant you understanding of the processes through which He draws you to Himself. Amen!

Augusta Ogbene
Asaba, Delta State
Nigeria

1 God's Building

God's Word beautifully portrays God's relationship to us in the light of what the eagle does. The phrase, "As an eagle, so the Lord" is a point of great importance and focus all through the pages of this book.

God is mysterious. And Solomon, the wisest man who ever lived, also talked about a few mysteries that were beyond his understanding. One of them, he said, was *"the way of an eagle in the air;"* (Proverbs 30:19). Little wonder that Scripture compares the outworking of God in our lives to the operation of this wonderful bird.

THE EAGLE'S NEST

As an eagle builds, so the Lord builds. In essence, as an eagle builds its nest, so the Lord builds our lives and circumstances. This being the case, it is important to understand how the eagle builds its nest.

First, nesting behaviour starts with some clearing out any unwanted debris and fixing any damaged areas around the nesting region.

God also begins the journey of building His people by clearing the debris around their lives and making them people worthy of His building. That is why 2Corinthians 5:17 says, *" Therefore if any man be in Christ, he is a*

Dr. Augusta Ogbene

new creature: old things are passed away; behold, all things are become new." But before this newness, something happened that helped clear the debris to get the man's life ready to be built by God.

In 1Corinthians 6:9-10, the Apostle Paul describes the lifestyle of the unsaved man before meeting Jesus:

Be not deceived: neither fornicators, nor idolaters, nor adulterers, nor effeminate, nor abusers of themselves with mankind, Nor thieves, nor covetous, nor drunkards, nor revilers, nor extortioners, shall inherit the kingdom of God." *He concludes by saying, "And such were some of you..(verse 11).*

The question is, if we ever were like this, what happened to us? Paul says, *"but ye are washed, but ye are sanctified, but ye are justified in the name of the Lord Jesus, and by the Spirit of our God"* (1Corinthians 6:11).

Dr. Augusta Ogbene

You see, like the eagle, God begins His building process with washing or cleansing the sinner with the precious Blood of Jesus. He first clears the debris then builds.

Second, it is important to understand that the eagle does not build around low terrains. It builds its nest in a tree or a rocky place high above the ground. The eagle builds so far high above the distraction and destruction of other living creatures. That way, the mother eagle is certain of the preservation of her eaglets.

Like the eagle God also builds the lives of His people far above the highest altitude that could ever be, way beyond the physical.

When we receive Jesus Christ as our personal Lord and Saviour, God does not only wash away our sins with the Blood of Jesus, He raises us up and sits us in heavenly places with Christ Jesus, *"far above all*

Dr. Augusta Ogbene

principality, and power, and might, and dominion, and every name that is named, not only in this world, but also in that which is to come:"(Ephesians 1:21).

Furthermore, apart from the preservation of the eaglets, the eagle builds far above the ground because she wants her little babies to have a mountain top experience as they grow and begin to learn how to fly.

In the same vein, beyond the preservation of their lives, God expects His people to have mountain top experiences in their relationship with Him. Have you ever had a "mountaintop experience" with God?

Think deeply about it:

God gave His covenant to Noah on Mount Ararat when the ark came to rest there after the flood.

Dr. Augusta Ogbene

God provided a ram for Abraham as a substitute for Isaac on Mount Moriah.

Moses had an amazing meeting with God on Mount Sinai, where he received the Ten Commandments.

Elijah defeated the prophets of Baal on Mount Carmel.

Jesus Himself was transfigured on a mountain, where Moses and Elijah joined him as Peter, James, and John looked on with awe.

Do you think these occurrences were mere coincidences? No! Like the mother eagle, God is interested in His people having as many mountaintop experiences as possible in their relationship with Him.

The famous evangelist Billy Graham had a life-changing encounter in a mountaintop

Dr. Augusta Ogbene

experience. Innumerable young people, pastors, evangelists, etc., have had life-changing encounters with the Lord at Christian camps or personal retreats in the mountains.

But is it all about climbing up a mountain to meet with God? No! It's rather the act of separation unto God for a time. It is at such times that the Lord builds the men He intends to use to mould the destinies of nations and generations.

Third, a typical nesting landscape for an eagle would be a forest of really tall trees and include rivers or lakes that offer areas of shallow water.

These landscapes provide for basic needs: water to drink, fish to eat, forest trees for shelter and a place to raise young, and perches for hunting and resting. In essence, the eagle builds where all it takes to nourish her young is available.

Dr. Augusta Ogbene

Again, as the eagle so the Lord builds. He brings the recreated new man into an environment where he can be built in prayer, in His Word, in character and integrity and in the experience of the warmth of fellowship.

This place is no other but His church. It is here that he makes His people lie down in green pastures and leads them beside still waters.

Jesus said, "*I am the door: by me if any man enter in, he shall be saved, and shall go in and out, and find pasture*" (John 10:9). The church is the Bride and Body of Christ, the embodiment of all that God offers His people through the Spirit of grace.

It is in the church that God nourishes and trains men for the task He has called them to accomplish.

Dr. Augusta Ogbene

Acts 13:2 says, "*As they ministered to the Lord, and fasted, the Holy Ghost said, Separate me Barnabas and Saul for the work whereunto I have called them.*" So, the Lord does not just build men in isolation, but mostly as a part of His Body, to fulfill His will and purposes.

Paul tells us in the Book of Ephesians that God trains, builds, and raises apostles, prophets, evangelists, pastors and teachers, "*for the perfecting of the saints, for the work of the ministry, for the edifying of the body of Christ:*" (Ephesians 4:12).

If you have given your life to Jesus Christ, you must belong to a specific Bible-based, Spirit-led church family where you can receive spiritual nourishment to grow thereby.

Fourth, the eagle usually starts by building small sized nests and then increase its size each year. Throughout the season, the eagle

Dr. Augusta Ogbene

keeps adding sticks to the nest, and continues to build on to them for many years.

This also portrays the way the Lord builds His people - from the smallest level of faith until He produces people of a strong and mature faith; people who can pull down strongholds and establish His authority wherever they find themselves.

Take a good look at the building of the Apostle Peter. Did he start out as a great apostle who addressed a crowd of people, raised a lame man to his feet and possessed shadows that healed the sick? Obviously not. He was a lay fisherman whom Jesus chose and patiently built into the great apostle he became.

Just like the eagle increases the size of its nest by adding to it time after time until it gets the desired size, God builds His men

Dr. Augusta Ogbene

through different situations and circumstances that adjust their life and character to become who He has always wanted them to be.

The Apostle Peter said, "*Ye also, as lively stones, are built up a spiritual house, an holy priesthood, to offer up spiritual sacrifices, acceptable to God by Jesus Christ*" (1 Peter 2:5).

Every sincere believer would agree that there has been a great level of improvement in their walk with God, different from when they started out.

It is because, like the eagle, God is constantly adding to the building (your life) to make it what He wants you to be. And He is still working on you, adding to you, changing you, and enlarging you.

Finally, the eagle never abandons its nest because of a misfortune. When an eagle

Dr. Augusta Ogbene

nest blows down, the eagle will usually build another nest nearby.

As the eagle, so the Lord builds His people. When His children, for one reason or the other, break down along the way, God never abandons them. He picks them up again and begins to rebuild them. He turns their mess into a message and makes something good out of a situation that would have seemingly crumbled them.

He said through Jeremiah, "*O house of Israel, cannot I do with you as this potter? saith the LORD. Behold, as the clay is in the potter's hand, so are ye in mine hand, O house of Israel*" (Jeremiah 18:6). God can always pick a battered life and revamp it into something new and beautiful just like the eagle would do her battered nest.

As the eagle, so the Lord builds!

Dr. Augusta Ogbene

God's Stirring

> *As an eagle stirreth up her nest,…so the LORD..* **Deuteronomy 32:11,12**

As the eagle, so the Lord breaks. The eagle is indeed a wonderful creature of God. The mother eagle makes her nest, and especially the part where the eggs will be laid as soft as possible. She lines it with softer materials and eagle feathers. That is where her young will be and there's need for some level of comfort.

Mother eagle knows, however, that her baby

eaglets were not born to stay in the nest for the rest of their lives. She cares for them and she longs to be near them. She is proud of them, but they were not born to stay in the nest, so she must do something to get them into becoming what they ought to be.

At first the mother eagle brings food right into the nest for her eaglets. But as the eaglets grow, food is no longer brought to their beak, but instead is dropped farther away, encouraging the eaglets to move about the nest and develop their food sourcing skills. As the eaglets move around the empty nest, exploring or gathering food, the process of strengthening their wings begins.

As they strengthen their wings the eaglets begin to learn what their side appendages can do. They become compelled to flap those side appendages to grasp the food. The awkward flapping of the wings further

Dr. Augusta Ogbene

strengthens their wings, preparing them for flight.

Similarly, as we will learn further on in this chapter, God uses our struggles as a means to strengthen us. Our suffering produces endurance, character, and hope. Romans 5:3(NLT) says, "We can rejoice, too, when we run into problems and trials, for we know that they help us develop endurance."

As the eaglets continue to grow, mother eagle returns to the nest less frequently and with less food. When she does return she begins to remove the comforts lining the nest. Yes, she worked really hard to build the nest, but she must begin to take away some parts of it, especially the soft things that make it so comfortable.

When the nest was built, mother eagle used thorns, broken branches, sharp rocks, and a number of other items that seem entirely

Dr. Augusta Ogbene

unsuitable for the project. But then she lined the nest with a thick padding of wool, feathers, and fur from animals she had killed, making it soft and comfortable for the eggs.

Because of the comfort of their nest and the luxury of free meals, the growing birds, even when they have reached flying age, are quite reluctant to leave. That is when the mother eagle begins stirring up the nest.

With her strong talons she begins pulling up the thick carpet of fur and feathers, bringing the sharp rocks and branches to the surface. As more of the bedding gets plucked up, the nest becomes more uncomfortable for the young eagles.

This mother eagle wants to cause her eaglets to look beyond the nest. She wants them to realize that they need to get out of there. She begins to break up the nest in little

Dr. Augusta Ogbene

steps. Bewildered, frustrated, and confused the eaglets move and begin to test out their wings out of desperation.

Mother eagle wisely knows that without this disruptive environment, her young will not grow, learn, and develop the essential skills needed for survival.

The eaglets do not understand at this time that the lack of food and removal of comfort are acts of tender care and love, a gift of provision by a loving mother who knows that without the ability to fly, they cannot survive and thrive.

Like the eagle, so the Lord stirs or breaks. Faith for the Christian is like flight for an eagle: essential to survive and thrive. But the process of developing faith is akin to the eaglet's training.

In the school of faith development, much like the eaglet bewildered by her parents, we

Dr. Augusta Ogbene

may be bewildered by our Father's actions (or lack thereof). We may even feel our Father has forgotten us, abandoned us, or withheld good from us. Yet, the Lord is tenderly developing our faith.

It may feel painful, and confusing, but in stirring our nest, our Heavenly Father is actually developing our hearts, our faith, and our patience in the wilderness of life.

The truth is, every Christian, if asked, would prefer a life with little or no resistance. We are more content with comfort and ease.

Actually, like the eaglets, when we first come to know the Lord, He provides us with all peace and comfort. Every prayer receives an almost immediate answer. Every cry is attended to with so much consolation and compensation. Everything just seems to flow from the throne of grace without any hesitation whatsoever.

Dr. Augusta Ogbene

But it does not continue like that all through life.

Like the mother eagle, with time, God begins to take away the sticks and the feathers that provide comfort. He begins to stir up and to break the nest of comfort and ease.

Do you wonder why things happen you never expected? Do you wonder why you face some difficulties? Do you wonder why things are not going smoothly for you as they once were?
God is shaking the nest. And that is because He wants to do more with your life than He has ever done before.

Anyone who has seen the mother eagle stir her nest or deal with her little eaglets will surely consider her cruel. While the eaglets are still in the nest right upon the rocky heights, the mother eagle comes and, taking

Dr. Augusta Ogbene

hold of them, flings them right out of the nest, high above the earth. They begin to fall straightway.

If you think only about the fate of the eaglets who have never been in air, you may never get the point. But when you think about what the mother eagle does after she throws out her young from that comfortable nest, you begin to gain understanding.

Having stirred up her nest, mother eagle spreads abroad her wings. While the poor tiny eagles struggle and fall, she swoops beneath them, catches them on her wings, and bears them up.

She did not cast them out of the nest in anger or wickedness. She was actually teaching them to fly. She wanted them to learn how to beat against the currents of the wind. So, having done that once, she drops them again, and again they struggle in the

Dr. Augusta Ogbene

air, but this time not so helplessly. They are finding out what she means. She spreads her pinions to show them how to fly, and as they fall again, she catches them again.

As the eagle, so the Lord deals with each of us. Has God been stirring up your nest recently? Has He flung you out and you feel so lost in a situation that is completely new and strange? Look up to Him and see that He is watching out for you. He is the Master of circumstances.

Watch! He is spreading out the wings of His omnipotence to bear you, to teach you how to soar above the winds and the waves - the adverse situations and circumstances of life. God will never allow you fall to the ground. He will always come beneath and catch you on His wings.

That is why He said, *"When thou passest through the waters, I will be with thee; and*

Dr. Augusta Ogbene

through the rivers, they shall not overflow thee: when thou walkest through the fire, thou shalt not be burned; neither shall the flame kindle upon thee" (Isaiah 43:2).

At first, you may think it is cruel and unkind for Him to fling you out of the nest, your comfort zone. No, He is merely teaching you to fly, that you might enter into all that He has promised you.

Like the little eagles, God wants you to mount up with wings that can beat against the wild currents of the winds of life. Little wonder that the Bible says, "*But they that wait upon the LORD shall renew their strength; they shall mount up with wings as eagles...*" (Isaiah 40:31a).

Few believers understand that to mount up with wings as eagles includes a breaking up of their comfort zone by the Hands of the Almighty.

Dr. Augusta Ogbene

No one wakes out of sleep to mount up with wings as eagles. You must experience the winds before the wings. Like the mother eagle, God does the work of casting His men into the harsh winds of life, so that they can build the muscles necessary to bear the visions and callings of tomorrow.

God does all He needs to do so we can learn how to use the gifts He has bestowed on us, and which we cannot use as long as we are in the nest.

Never forget that the Israelites spent forty years in the wilderness facing different situations and circumstances beyond their expectations. That journey actually had other advantages besides leading them to Canaan. The long marches and desert sands developed powers of endurance which had lain dormant amid the fleshpots of Egypt.

There are in you faculties and energies

Dr. Augusta Ogbene

imprisoned or bottled up, which will show up when your nest - your comfort zone - is broken up.

You see, it is beautiful and fanciful to behold the eaglets in the nest. But it is contrary to their nature and the purposes for which they were created. They were meant to fly upward. Keeping them in the nest will not fulfill that purpose.

The nest will turn them into mere chicken that was meant only to walk the earth. The stirring is therefore, of utmost necessity, to usher them into their purpose.
Beloved, God has a purpose for your life, and He wants you to fulfill it. If you stop in the nest, you will never get there.

That is why God comes into your life, shakes you up and out of your comfort zone, breaks up your little, feeble, self-centred plans, and extinguishes your carnal hopes. He seemingly spoils everything that

Dr. Augusta Ogbene

has brought you joy and happiness or keeps them from you for a time.

What's all that for?

That He may get you on His wings, teach you the secret forces of your own life, and lead you to the higher purposes for which He made you.

Pain and troubles in your life are His "wake-up call" to motivate and move you out of your comfort zone, to grow towards your God-given potential and become all that He envisioned for you to be and to do all that He wants you to do.

Take a look at Israel, God's prized possession. They are a good picture of how the Lord God breaks His people to achieve His purpose for their lives. God had spoken to Abraham that his descendants will become slaves in a strange land and in due time, He would set them free.

Dr. Augusta Ogbene

He said, "*Know of a surety that thy seed shall be a stranger in a land that is not theirs, and shall serve them; and they shall afflict them four hundred years;*" (Genesis 15:13).

Nevertheless, when seventy souls from Jacob's household went down into Egypt (Genesis 47:6), their cattle throve, they had fine possessions, and a monarch's favour. Life was so beautiful for them in a choice land in Egypt.

With the passage of time, Joseph died and his services were soon forgotten. The once favoured children of Israel came to be regarded as slaves and workmen for the king of Egypt. They were badly abused and set to hard labour.

God allowed their nest to become so uncomfortable towards the close of the four hundred and thirty years in Goshen, that they resolved to try their wings.

Dr. Augusta Ogbene

For the first time in years, the children of Israel learned how to pray, to cry out to their Maker - the God of their fathers - for help. The Bible says, "*And it came to pass in process of time, that...the children of Israel sighed by reason of the bondage, and they cried, and their cry came up unto God by reason of the bondage*" (Exodus 2:23).

The truth is, if things had continued as usual, the children of Israel would never really know the God of their fathers. They probably would never know what it means to pray or call upon the Lord for help. But when they were shaken out of their comfort zone, they learned how to make demands on the help of God.

Beloved, do you know that there are wealthy men and women who learned how to pray for the first time only in the face of calamity?

Do you know that there are many believers

Dr. Augusta Ogbene

who never knew what it means to fast and pray until God allowed them to contact adverse situations that were beyond human psychology and medical intervention?

Without a stirred, shaken or broken nest, many would never know God beyond "Creator."

And truth be told, if God did not stir up some people's nests, they would sink down into utter worldliness.

Today, some have known Jehovah as the Lord that heals because they experienced a sickness which was beyond medical science but was healed only by Jehovah Ropheka, the Almighty Healer.

Some people now know God as deliverer because they had been through hell in the hands of the enemy and found solution in nothing else but the power of the Almighty God.

Dr. Augusta Ogbene

Without some of these situations, many would never understand the Almightiness of God or even think of living in reverence of Him. Their pain, troubles, and trials brought them to maturity in God and His ways.

You see, one of the purposes of trial, of trouble, of sorrow, and of tribulation, is to make us grow unto maturity. Somehow without trouble and without trial, the soul never matures. Hebrews 2:10 says, *"For it became Him, God . . . to make the captain of our salvation perfect through sufferings."*

The word "perfect" used here does not imply "freedom from sin," for our Lord never sinned. He was never imperfect. The word "perfect" here means "maturity" or "grown up." It means to reach the goal for which it was intended. The Lord Jesus was made to reach His intended destiny through suffering.

Dr. Augusta Ogbene

The Bible tells us that "*Though He were a Son, yet learned He obedience by the things which He suffered*" (Hebrews 5:8). We grow to maturity by going through the trials of life. The disciplines of our earthly pilgrimage are given us of God, that we might grow unto maturity in Him. Without those disciplines and trials, we are weak and anemic.

Countless testimonies abound to the discovery of purpose after people survived encounters that they thought would crumble them forever. Many great Ministries have been birthed from such encounters.

Beloved, don't take for granted the difficulties you experience in life, Ministry, marriage, school, or wherever you find yourself. You may be the one your generation is waiting for, and what you face today can be key to fulfilling your destiny. The testing of your faith is the opportunity to lay solid foundations for the future.

Dr. Augusta Ogbene

The Bible says, "*For you know that when your faith is tested, your endurance has a chance to grow. So let it grow, for when your endurance is fully developed, you will be perfect and complete, needing nothing*" (James 1:3-4, NLT).

Like gold, there is a purpose in the fire, the sorrow, the trial, and the discipline. God is training you to become all He planned for you to be and do.

In conclusion, I'll say blessed be the discipline, however painful or severe, that stirs up our nests and teaches us to live as sons and daughters of the Almighty God and heirs of our unfading crown!

Please pray with me for a minute: "*Dear Lord God, in all the trials and troubles You allow to come into my life, please help me use them as an opportunity to grow, so that I will become 'strong in character and ready for anything.' Thank You Father. In Jesus' Name, amen.*"

Dr. Augusta Ogbene

3 God's Fluttering

> *As an eagle...that fluttereth over her young,...So the LORD...* **Deuteronomy 32:11,12**

As an eagle, so the Lord flutters or broods. To flutter is to fly unsteadily or hover by flapping the wings quickly and lightly.

The eagle flutters or broods over her young. In fluttering she provides protection, warmth and reassurance for her growing eaglets. It is important to know why the eagle flutters over her young after stirring the nest because it'll greatly help in understanding how the Lord works with His people.

In the last chapter, we saw how the mother eagle provides food and comfort for her young. Her acts of tenderness make the eaglets so comfortable and at ease. But as they grow she tries to get them to grow out of that comfort zone in order to become the eagles they are meant to be and not chicks.

For a time, the eaglets have known their mother to be very loving and tender. They enjoy that warmth of parenting until the days when mother comes home without food.

As if that isn't enough, mother comes back some other day and begins to tear away all the soft materials in the nest that supplied their comfort. Things begin to get so rough. But that is not where it ends.

Dr. Augusta Ogbene

Mother finally comes on a certain day and begins to push them out of the nest into the wild winds that they are not familiar with.

The eaglets begin to get confused. Why was mother so caring and then suddenly becomes so cruel? What have they done wrong? Unknown to them, it is not about what they have done wrong but what they need to do right. Mother is doing all these things to help them become who they ought to be.

After the training sessions are over, mother eagle understands the mixed feelings in the minds of her young. She comes over to where they are and tries to show them the love and tenderness she is well known for.

She lets them know that she still loves and cares for them, and is always there to protect them. She spreads open her wings and covers them with it to reassure them of her presence, protection and care.

Dr. Augusta Ogbene

All her seriousness in the few moments past was just a way of getting their attention in order to train them for the next level.

As the eagle, so the Lord flutters over His own. He said in Psalms 125:2 says, "*As the mountains are round about Jerusalem, so the LORD is round about his people from henceforth even for ever.*"

The Lord protects His people and covers them under His tender loving wings. Psalms 91:4 reiterates this when it says, "*He will cover thee with his feathers and under his wings shalt thou trust.*"

Like the eagle, God has to do this because it is easy for humans, feeble as they are, to get confused and terrified after the Lord shakes their nest.

At a certain point in the difficulties they face, most men stop and ask themselves, "Where is God in all of this?"

Dr. Augusta Ogbene

Israel was at that point too. The Bible tells us that God sent plagues that shook Egypt but never affected the Israelites. He took them through the Red Sea on dry ground and did many other marvelous miracles before them. But the time came when He stirred their nest. He allowed them experience some things they didn't expect.

When Israel got to that point, they became totally confused. They wondered why the God Who has been so tender and loving towards them had suddenly become so cold and numb in their direction.

They began to imagine that He had abandoned them. The Bible says Moses *"called the name of the place Massah, and Meribah, because of the chiding of the children of Israel, and because they tempted the LORD, saying, Is the LORD among us, or not?"*

Most men come to that point at least once in

Dr. Augusta Ogbene

their lifetime. Others experience it at different points in their lives.

Let me ask you beloved, have you ever been in a situation where you prayed all the prayers you knew and walked in all the godly counsel and suggestions you were given, yet there were no visible results?

Have you ever been at that point of thirst, like the Israelites experienced, where water was not at sight and couldn't even be expected? That is, what you wanted was not within reach and there was no hope of getting it either. It happens in every man's life.

But God is faithful.

Knowing how frail the sons of men are, like the mother eagle, God has to brood or flutter over them after a moment of shaking the nest of their lives. The Bible says in

Dr. Augusta Ogbene

Psalms 103:14 (NLT), *"For he knows how weak we are; he remembers we are only dust."*

God knows just how much you can take. To the church in Philadelphia Jesus said, *"for thou hast a little strength,.."* (Revelations 3:8).

God knows the point beyond which you might be totally broken, and He will never stretch you to that extent.

Everything you have gone through up to this point in your life, are within the limits of your capabilities. God will never allow what will consume you to confront you.

After a period of shaking, the Father lovingly flutters over His own. He stretches forth His hand and pulls you into the warmth of His embrace, just to let you know He was there all the time.

I believe it was in this light that the songwriter wrote,

Dr. Augusta Ogbene

Jesus could see through the walls I had built round my heart;
He was acquainted with grief that had torn me apart;
He reached out to hold me, to touch me, console me again;
The teardrops would stop at simply the touch of His hand.

I gazed in the mirror, and I can't believe what I see;
Reflections of laughter where all of the pain used to be;
It seems like a lifetime, but I see the sunshine at last;
And I sure love the thrill, now that the storm has passed.

Beloved, the truth is, you would never know the feeling of the everlasting arms of a Heavenly Father lifting you and saving you from destruction, fear, and burdens unless God stirs your nest every once in a while.

Dr. Augusta Ogbene

And though you experience His stirring, you must understand that it's not going to last a lifetime.

You know, when you experience a shaking of your nest, it is easy for people to look at you as one whom God has forsaken. It's easy for people to hate, despise, and make all manner of unnecessary remarks about you.

But as much as you respond positively to His stirring, the Father of all spirits will surely flutter over you again. He will smile over you again and make you the envy of many. He said, "*Whereas thou hast been forsaken and hated,…I will make thee an eternal excellency, a joy of many generations*" (Isaiah 60:15).

I NEED YOUR ATTENTION

Picture in your mind what happens in the nest after mother eagle has shaken the

Dr. Augusta Ogbene

eaglets out, trained them a bit and brought them back in. After the entire experience, the young eagles cling to their mother a bit more than usual. They turn their entire attention to her. They have passed through something they never experienced before.

There is a mix of fear, excitement and anxiety in their heart. Now they all cling to their mother for warmth and reassurance. In a moment, mother eagle has the attention of all her young. Now she can tell them whatever she wills and they're ready to listen.

Many times, we get so comfortable with the provisions of God that we unknowingly become spiritually complacent in some way. Everything moves so smoothly that we exclude God from our routines without knowing.

God tries in many ways to get our attention

Dr. Augusta Ogbene

to no avail. A lot of times, He has to shake or break our nests in order to get our focus back on Him.

Listen! Many of the so-called problems in the lives of men are simply God's way of getting their attention. The problem is, rather than give Him the attention He seeks, most men begin to run here and there seeking help from prayer houses, pastors, prophets, etc.

But you see, no man can quench a fire God starts. No one can solve a problem God permits. No man, no matter his level of anointing, can help a person God is working on.

If some pastors had more knowledge, they would refer most people back to God rather than try to play God in the issues of such people.

Dr. Augusta Ogbene

If some prophets knew, they would refer some people back to God rather than try to see what God is not showing them about such people.

If some doctors knew, they would refer some cases back to God rather than try to complicate issues in such lives. Cases that God institutes can only be handled by God.

If God has allowed a situation in your life in order to get your attention, you must give Him that attention if you truly need a way out.

The tragedy is that a lot of people live on with their situations and even progress from bad to worse because it never occurs to them that it might be God seeking their attention, so something can be corrected.

That was the case with Israel. They went from bad to worse each day, because rather

Dr. Augusta Ogbene

than give God the attention He sought, they resorted to murmuring against Him. And they never survived it, for He wasted all of them in the wilderness.

You tell me you have moved from one form of confusion to another, and I ask you, is God trying to get your attention? Will you give Him that attention? God will do anything in His mercy to get your attention.

In shaking the comfort zone you have created for yourself, He may allow or permit suffering, sickness, adversity, anguish, trials, tribulations, and heartaches in your life. This is truth so hard to pass across.

Note that it is not God's will that we go through life from one crisis to another. No! He loves us deeply and wants us to build our life on a solid foundation which is founded on the truth of His Holy Word. As a matter of fact, if God didn't love us, He wouldn't bother trying to get our attention.

Dr. Augusta Ogbene

Our Heavenly Father wants us to understand that we need Him, or that we constantly need His guidance and direction in life.

There are disappointing, heartbreaking things that happen sometimes to turn our eyes back on the Son of God. And the beauty of it is that His eyes are always on us.

THINK ABOUT ASA

Asa was the third king of Judah after Solomon. He was the son and successor of Abijam. 1Kings 15:8 says, "*And Abijam slept with his fathers; and they buried him in the city of David: and Asa his son reigned in his stead.*"

Asa began to reign B.C. 951, and reigned forty-one years at Jerusalem. The first part of his reign was comparatively peaceful and prosperous. The Bible says in 1Kings 15:11 that "*Asa did that which was right in the eyes of the LORD, as did David his father.*"

Dr. Augusta Ogbene

Asa restored the pure worship of God, expelled those who prostituted themselves in honour of their false gods; purified Jerusalem from the infamous practices attending the worship of idols; and deprived his mother of her office and dignity of queen, because she erected an idol to Astarte.

The Bible says, "*Asa's heart was perfect with the LORD all his days*" (1Kings 15:14). Things went all well until God stirred Asa's nest to move him to the next level in his relationship with Him.

God wanted to rebuild and intensify Asa's trust in Him, which was already beginning to wane. The Bible says, "*And there was war between Asa and Baasha king of Israel all their days. And Baasha king of Israel went up against Judah, and built Ramah, that he might not suffer any to go out or come in to Asa king of Judah*" (1Kings 15:16-17).

Dr. Augusta Ogbene

This was not the first time Asa had experienced war or threat. In the eleventh year of his reign, the Bible says,

And there came out against them Zerah the Ethiopian with an host of a thousand thousand, and three hundred chariots; and came unto Mareshah. Then Asa went out against him, and they set the battle in array in the valley of Zephathah at Mareshah. And Asa cried unto the LORD his God, and said, LORD, it is nothing with thee to help, whether with many, or with them that have no power: help us, O LORD our God; for we rest on thee, and in thy name we go against this multitude. O LORD, thou art our God; let not man prevail against thee. So the LORD smote the Ethiopians before Asa, and before Judah; and the Ethiopians fled (2Chronicles 14:9-12).

God gave Asa the victory over the vast army of the Cushite king Zerah; and the prophet Azariah encouraged him to go on in his

Dr. Augusta Ogbene

work of reform. The prophet said, *"Be ye strong therefore, and let not your hands be weak: for your work shall be rewarded"* (2Chronicles 15:7). Yet, when Baasha king of Israel opposed his work, Asa sought aid not from God, but from heathen Syria.

Asa's trust in God was waning and God already knew this, hence the need for a stirring. Asa had enjoyed victories by the supernatural Hand but was beginning to get complacent in his relationship with his Helper. God needed to stir his nest and get back his attention, but Asa was too engrossed with himself to notice this.

When God couldn't get king Asa's attention, He sent a seer to him to help him get back on track.

2Chronicles 16:7-9 says, *"And at that time Hanani the seer came to Asa king of Judah, and said unto him, Because thou hast relied on the*

Dr. Augusta Ogbene

king of Syria, and not relied on the LORD thy God, therefore is the host of the king of Syria escaped out of thine hand. Were not the Ethiopians and the Lubims a huge host, with very many chariots and horsemen? yet, because thou didst rely on the LORD, he delivered them into thine hand. For the eyes of the LORD run to and fro throughout the whole earth, to shew himself strong in the behalf of them whose heart is perfect toward him. Herein thou hast done foolishly: therefore from henceforth thou shalt have wars."

This message was not meant to get king Asa angry; it was meant to help him see how much he had unknowingly drifted away in the matter of his trust in God. But the king did not see it that way.

The Bible says, *"Then Asa was wroth with the seer, and put him in a prison house; for he was in a rage with him because of this thing"* (2Chronicles 16:10). God could not get

Dr. Augusta Ogbene

Asa's attention through the seer's message. So, He had to find another way.

God stretched onto Asa's health. The Bible says, "*And Asa in the thirty and ninth year of his reign was diseased in his feet, until his disease was exceeding great:*" (2Chronicles 16:12a).

This disease was not meant to destroy Asa. It was meant to draw his attention to the God who so helped him, but whom he had forsaken. Asa would not understand still.

In Psalms 32:9 the Lord said, "*Be ye not as the horse, or as the mule, which have no understanding: whose mouth must be held in with bit and bridle, …*" But that is exactly how king Asa was. He refused to understand every step God took to regain his attention.

The Bible says, "*yet in his disease he sought not to the LORD, but to the physicians*" (2Chronicles 16:12a).

Dr. Augusta Ogbene

Even in such a terribly diseased state, Asa went to the doctors rather seek God. He still missed the point.

How could a doctor cure a disease permitted by God? Is there any drug in the world that can dry up a wound God opens?

Finally Asa died in a bad state. He didn't have to, but unfortunately he did.

DON'T GET THERE

The story of Asa is just one out of many. There are a lot more examples of such all through Scripture. But the point is, you don't really need to get to where Asa got. No; you don't need to get there.

When God stirred Asa's nest using Baasha king of Israel, it was for the good of king Asa. It was to help him shoot up his trust in God which was already waning slowly.

Dr. Augusta Ogbene

His failure to turn to God for help in the face of Baasha's attack was enough opportunity to cry out to God to help restore his trust in Him.

The visit of the seer was another good opportunity to humbly turn to God, admit his failure and rebuild strength.

The disease in his feet was yet another great opportunity to rebuild his trust in God.

Taking any of these opportunities would have afforded Asa the privilege of experiencing God's fluttering – His consolation, embrace, warmth and reassurance.

But Asa wouldn't take all the opportunities God offered him. He was like the mule; he wouldn't understand God's moves. God's intent was never to kill him, for he was a good-hearted man, but he died of a total lack of understanding.

Dr. Augusta Ogbene

Switch a bit from Asa and take a look at Jonah whose action was the exact opposite of Asa's. When God sent Jonah to Nineveh, he took off to Tarshish. On his way, there was a serious storm. Jonah knew that the storm was not meant to kill him, but rather get his attention back on what God had called him to do.

While in the belly of the fish, Jonah responded to God positively and also received the Master's fluttering.

But how? you ask.

Well, remember that when Jonah ran into the ship going to Tarshish, he paid his fare for the journey all by himself. But when he repented in the belly of the fish, he didn't need to pay his way to Nineveh anymore, for God caused the fish to transport him to that city free of charge.

Dr. Augusta Ogbene

Jonah didn't have to lose his life in the belly of the fish because he understood God's moves immediately. He knew why the nest was stirred and responded accordingly.

GOD WILL ALWAYS FLUTTER

When the nest is stirred, the Heavenly Father wants you to respond positively.

Find out what He is drawing your attention to. Listen to your spirit. Get a solitary place where you can communicate with your Father and hear Him speak deep within you.

He said, *"I will instruct thee and teach thee in the way which thou shalt go: I will guide thee with mine eye"*(Psalms 32:8). Find out His instructions and receive His guidance.

After a period of stirring, God always sees to it that He flutters over His own. The stirring

Dr. Augusta Ogbene

may seem horrible, but His fluttering restores, revives, revitalizes, rebuilds, re-energizes and recreates.

No matter what you have to face, God is always there to brood over you and take care of you. The important thing is that you learn what He wanted you to learn and grow in your experience rather than degenerate in it.

The song writer asked,

Does Jesus care when my heart is pained
Too deeply for mirth and song,
As the burdens press and the cares distress,
And the way grows weary and long?

O yes, He cares, I know He cares,
His heart is touched with my grief;
When the days are weary, the long night dreary,
I know my Savior cares.

Dr. Augusta Ogbene

4 God's Bearing

One of the most magnificent things about the eagle is the way it spreads across her large wings to take and to bear her young.

Why does mother or father eagle do this?

We already learned in a previous chapter that this is the way they train the eaglets to fly. Apart from this, however, there are other reasons the eagle spreads its wings to take and to bear its young.

IN WEARINESS

The eagle spreads abroad her wings, not only to teach the young ones how to fly, but also to bear them when they are weary. Getting into the air at thousands of feet above sea level can be very demanding for young eaglets. As they struggle to flap their wings in air, they get weary in no time.

Mother eagle is constantly watching to see what happens to them. Once she realizes that her little ones are becoming weary and are beginning to drift with the winds, she swoops under them, spreads her wings and takes them in order to let them have some rest and renew their strength.

Like the eagle, so the Lord bears His people. As earlier stated, God knows the limits of each person's strength. He knows that all men are feeble, to say the least, and He knows how easily they get weary in the journey of life.

Dr. Augusta Ogbene

When He finds His loving children weak and weary, He swoops under them like the eagle and takes them on His great wings. He bears them there until they regain the strength to continue.

Let me ask you beloved, have you never been tired in this race? Have you never been discouraged? Have you never felt like giving up at some point? Have you never been in a position where prayer was tiring, the appetite to study God's Word was gone, and spirituality in general was difficult? Have you never been so tired that you slept off without praying?

If you are a preacher, have you never felt at anytime, that if you weren't the one preaching, you would have stayed back from attending that service?

We often grow weary somewhere, somehow. Many times our strength fails us.

Dr. Augusta Ogbene

The Psalmist said, *"My flesh and my heart faileth: but God is the strength of my heart,…"* (Psalms 76:26).

Many times we don't feel like getting on. We feel like having a little holiday or spiritual vacation. At such times, our Father understands our weariness and lovingly spreads His wings to take and to bear us. That is why the Bible says, *"He giveth power to the faint; and to them that have no might he increaseth strength"* (Isaiah 40:29).

When does He give power and increase strength? When He takes us on His wings and bears us there.

Jesus reiterated this when He said, *"Come unto me, all ye that labour and are heavy laden, and I will give you rest"* (Matthew 11:28). The metaphor here appears to be taken from a man who has a great load laid upon him, which he must carry to a certain place.

Dr. Augusta Ogbene

Every step he takes reduces his strength and renders his load heavier on him. But because he must carry it, he labours and uses his utmost strength to move towards his destination.

Life is full of loads and burdens. While we try to serve the Lord, we are faced with challenges that drain our inner strength. Sometimes we just have to be very strong to forge ahead. But every step ahead tends to reduce our strength.

In addition to personal burdens, we come in contact with so-called Christian folks who do to us what many unbelievers would never do. They make our hearts heavy and our souls weary.

David said, "*For it was not an enemy that reproached me; then I could have borne it: neither was it he that hated me that did magnify himself against me; then I would have hid myself from*

Dr. Augusta Ogbene

him: But it was thou, a man mine equal, my guide, and mine acquaintance. We took sweet counsel together, and walked unto the house of God in company" (Psalms 55:12-14).

When these things happen, they break us. They sap our strength. They become burdens we never expected to bear. But it is at such times that the Master spreads His wings to take us, bear us, hold us and console us again.

Are you tired, weak and weary? Is your strength already consumed by the burdens you bear? Is no one willing to give a listening ear or even try to understand your plight?

Don't worry, there's Someone Who hears the whispers of your heart; Someone Who's more than willing to take you up on His wings, bear you and strengthen you again. Just wait upon Him, for *"they that wait upon*

Dr. Augusta Ogbene

the LORD shall renew their strength; they shall mount up with wings as eagles; they shall run, and not be weary; and they shall walk, and not faint" (Isaiah 40:31).

Are you a sinner wearied in the ways of iniquity? Jesus also invites you to come to Him and find speedy relief. Are you a backslider burdened with the guilt of your compromises and secret sin? You are invited to come to the Sacrifice of the Saviour and find instant pardon.

FROM THE ARCHER'S EYE

Is there any other reason why the eagle bears the young on its wings?

Yes, there is.

The eagle takes the eaglets upon her back so that the archers cannot injure them. For any archer to injure the young bird, it must first

Dr. Augusta Ogbene

pierce through the body of the mother to reach them.

Paul tried to explain this when he said, "*For ye are dead, and your life is hid with Christ in God*" (Colossians 3:3). In essence, Paul was telling the believers in Colosse that any arrow that has to reach them must first pierce through Jesus Christ the Master and God the Father. But that is impossible!

The Psalmist captured this attribute of God when he said, "*Yea, though I walk through the valley of the shadow of death, I will fear no evil: for thou art with me;*" (Psalms 23:4).

God covers, protects and preserves His own. There is no need to worry or fear. The battle may be raging, but the victory is sure. You are protected from the archer's eye by the wings of the Father.

David said, "*For in the time of trouble he shall*

Dr. Augusta Ogbene

hide me in his pavilion: in the secret of his tabernacle shall he hide me;" (Psalms 27:5). And no devil can find the one whom God hides.

This was the role God played in the lives of the Israelites when Balak hired Balaam to curse them. They made sacrifices on several places, but Israel remained invisible to the eyes of the enemy. No matter what they did, it was simply impossible to destroy the people whom God had securely covered under the shadows of His wings.

After several attempts, Balaam came to one conclusion: *"Surely there is no enchantment against Jacob, neither is there any divination against Israel."* (Numbers 23:23). The New Living Translation makes it more vivid: *"No curse can touch Jacob; no magic has any power against Israel."*

Beloved, do not be threatened by the harsh

Dr. Augusta Ogbene

pronouncements of the wicked. There is no enchantment against the man that is borne on the wings of the Most High. You cannot be cursed. You cannot be destroyed. You cannot be sent to an early grave. Your Ministry cannot be cut short. You cannot be made to see shame or reproach when the Lord of Hosts bears you securely on His wings.

God's Word to you on this is sure: *"For I, saith the LORD, will be unto her a wall of fire round about, and will be the glory in the midst of her"* (Zechariah 2:5). And do you know, beloved that, *"he that toucheth you toucheth the apple of his eye"*? (Zechariah 2:8)

No devil can dare the one whom God bears. Relax! You have been raised above the archer's eyes. You are seated with Christ in heavenly places far above principalities and powers, and your life is hidden with Christ in God.

Dr. Augusta Ogbene

RECOUNTING THE BLESSINGS

Nehemiah recounted a few blessings of God bearing His people on His wings. He said in Nehemiah 9:19-25,

19 ...the pillar of the cloud departed not from them by day, to lead them in the way; neither the pillar of fire by night, to shew them light, and the way wherein they should go.
20 Thou gavest also thy good spirit to instruct them, and withheldest not thy manna from their mouth, and gavest them water for their thirst.
21 Yea, forty years didst thou sustain them in the wilderness, so that they lacked nothing; their clothes waxed not old, and their feet swelled not.
22 Moreover thou gavest them kingdoms and nations, and didst divide them into corners: so they possessed the land of Sihon, and the land of the king of Heshbon, and the land of Og king of Bashan.
23 Their children also multipliedst thou as the stars of heaven, and broughtest them into the

Dr. Augusta Ogbene

land, concerning which thou hadst promised to their fathers, that they should go in to possess it.

24 So the children went in and possessed the land, and thou subduedst before them the inhabitants of the land, the Canaanites, and gavest them into their hands, with their kings, and the people of the land, that they might do with them as they would.

25 And they took strong cities, and a fat land, and possessed houses full of all goods, wells digged, vineyards, and oliveyards, and fruit trees in abundance: so they did eat, and were filled, and became fat, and delighted themselves in thy great goodness.

Earlier on, Moses had said to the Israelites, *"And I have led you forty years in the wilderness:* ***your clothes are not waxen old*** *upon you, and* ***thy shoe is not waxen old*** *upon thy foot"* (Deuteronomy 29:5).

But how could their clothes or shoes wax old when they were continually borne above the earth?

Dr. Augusta Ogbene

Again, to keep the picture fresh on their minds, God took the time to recount the blessings of bearing them on His wings all through their journeys. He said in Joshua 24:2-13,

"2 Your fathers dwelt on the other side of the flood in old time, even Terah, the father of Abraham, and the father of Nachor: and they served other gods.

3 And I took your father Abraham from the other side of the flood, and led him throughout all the land of Canaan, and multiplied his seed, and gave him Isaac.

4 And I gave unto Isaac Jacob and Esau: and I gave unto Esau mount Seir, to possess it; but Jacob and his children went down into Egypt.

5 I sent Moses also and Aaron, and I plagued Egypt, according to that which I did among them: and afterward I brought you out.

6 And I brought your fathers out of Egypt: and ye came unto the sea; and the Egyptians pursued after your fathers with chariots and horsemen

Dr. Augusta Ogbene

unto the Red sea.

7 And when they cried unto the Lord, he put darkness between you and the Egyptians, and brought the sea upon them, and covered them; and your eyes have seen what I have done in Egypt: and ye dwelt in the wilderness a long season.

8 And I brought you into the land of the Amorites, which dwelt on the other side Jordan; and they fought with you: and I gave them into your hand, that ye might possess their land; and I destroyed them from before you.

9 Then Balak the son of Zippor, king of Moab, arose and warred against Israel, and sent and called Balaam the son of Beor to curse you:

10 But I would not hearken unto Balaam; therefore he blessed you still: so I delivered you out of his hand.

11 And ye went over Jordan, and came unto Jericho: and the men of Jericho fought against you, the Amorites, and the Perizzites, and the Canaanites, and the Hittites, and the Girgashites, the Hivites, and the Jebusites; and I

Dr. Augusta Ogbene

delivered them into your hand.
12 And I sent the hornet before you, which drave them out from before you, even the two kings of the Amorites; but not with thy sword, nor with thy bow.
13 And I have given you a land for which ye did not labour, and cities which ye built not, and ye dwell in them; of the vineyards and oliveyards which ye planted not do ye eat".

God did all of the above and more, to prove to His people that He was involved in their lives and that He bore them on His wings. Space will fail me to recount more and more of the power of God in the lives of His people to prove that He was with them, bearing them on His wings, delivering them from uncertainty, unnecessary pain, and unwanted circumstances.

But I'd like you to know beloved, that the Wings that bore Israel in all the encounters we have recounted, also bears you. Glory hallelujah!

Dr. Augusta Ogbene

Are circumstances crashing down around you? Let not your heart be troubled. Listen closely, and you will hear the voice of the Master saying, *"Be still, and know that I am God"* (Psalms 46:10).

He is God! He was not more powerful yesterday. He will not be more powerful tomorrow. He is Jehovah Shammah - the ever present God. He is as powerful today as He has ever been, and He will show Himself strong in your behalf.

Open up and pour your heart before Him today. Make demands on the Wings that bore Israel through that lonely and terrible wilderness. Cast all your cares upon Him, for He cares for you.

May the words of the good old time hymn on the next page sink deep into the recesses of your being:

Dr. Augusta Ogbene

Hear the blessed Savior
calling the oppressed
Come ye heavy laden
come to me and rest
Come no longer tarry
I your load will bear
Bring me every burden
bring me every care

Come unto me
And I will give you rest
Take my yoke upon you
Hear me and be blessed
I am meek and lowly
Come and trust my might
Come (oh come)
my yoke is easy
And my burdens light

Are you disappointed, wandering here and there?
Dragging chains of doubt and
loaded down with care?
Do unholy feelings struggle in your breast?

Dr. Augusta Ogbene

Bring your case to Jesus
He will give you rest

Have you by temptation
often conquered been?
Has a sense of weakness
brought distress within?
Christ will sanctify you
if you claim His best
In the Holy Spirit
He will give you rest

Dr. Augusta Ogbene

> As an eagle stirreth up her nest, fluttereth over her young, spreadeth abroad her wings, taketh them, beareth them on her wings: So the LORD alone did lead him, **Deuteronomy 32:11, 12**

As we get to this point, we begin to see much clearly what the Lord is doing: why He is building His people; why He stirs their nests; why He flutters over them; why He spreads His wings to take and bear them.

It is all for one reason: So that **HE ALONE** can lead them! Everything God did for Israel from the beginning was for this singular reason. He wanted to be Lord of their lives. He wanted to be their leader.

He wanted them to get to that point where nothing else and no one else was of more importance than Himself.

In all of this, God was subtly saying to Israel, "I want you to understand what I am doing in your life. I want you to know Me. I want you to come unto Me. I want you to be exclusively mine."

He said to Israel in Exodus 19:4, "*Ye have seen what I did unto the Egyptians, and how I bare you on eagles' wings, and brought you unto myself.*" That was His ultimate desire – to bring them to Himself.

And He will raise you on eagles' wings
Bear you on the breath of dawn,
Make you to shine like the sun
And hold you in the palm of His hand
The snare of the flower will never capture you

Dr. Augusta Ogbene

And famine will bring you no fear,
Under His wings your refuge,
His faithfulness your shield

Michael Joncas

Beloved, God is building you, shaking you, fluttering over you, and bearing you, so He can lead you. All He wants is that He might have you all for Himself and guide you step-by-step through this wilderness of life.

But, you ask, why is God so interested in leading my life? There are quite a number of reasons but I'll share a few.

INTIMACY WITH HIM

As I've repeatedly said, one of the major reasons the Lord bore Israel on His wings was *to lead them to Himself*. He was not leading them to a land but to Himself. He said to the children of Israel, "*Ye have seen… how I bare you on eagles' wings, and brought you unto myself*" (Exodus 19:4).

Dr. Augusta Ogbene

God desires, more than anything else, to lead you to Himself. He desires intimacy with you. He said, "*This people have I formed for myself; they shall shew forth my praise*" (Isaiah 43:2).

Beloved, you were created to love, worship, serve and fellowship with your Maker. What God wants to do more than anything else, is draw you to Himself. He created you with a longing for intimacy - intimacy with Him. He desires and appreciates that intimacy, so He calls for it.

This is why God often came down to fellowship with man in the Garden of Eden. Genesis 3:8 tells how Adam and his wife heard "*the voice of the LORD God walking in the garden in the cool of the day:*"

It was the desire for intimacy that caused the LORD God to carve out a people for Himself, beginning with Abraham.

Dr. Augusta Ogbene

Through Abraham, Isaac and Jacob, He called Israel to be His own. Since then, He has worked intensely throughout time, to bring humanity back to a place of intimate communion, where He can share His heart with them and hear their hearts expressed to Him.

But why is God so desirous of leading you into intimacy with Him? Because He wants you to know Him!

Beloved, you cannot know someone you don't spend time with.

Intimacy results or develops from close contact with someone over a period of time. When there is such close contact, trust is built, confidence grows, and hearts become endeared to one another. This is what God desires.

Dr. Augusta Ogbene

YOU NEED PEACE

Have you ever been into something that brought you so much sorrow afterwards? Have you ever tried something that led to many regrets? Did you ever board a vehicle that ran into some form of mishap along the way?

Hear this: God wants to be in your life leading you daily to avoid painful errors, unnecessary sorrow, mishap, troubles and difficulties. When God is the leader of your life, you experience peace. And your peace is more important than many things you can think of.

Once peace is lost, health is lost. Once peace is lost, life becomes completely unbearable. If there's anything God wants you to have in the journey of life, it is peace. Jesus said in John 14:27, *"Peace I leave with you, my peace I give unto you. Let not your heart be troubled, neither let it be afraid."*

Dr. Augusta Ogbene

So how does God lead? Beside the still waters! The Psalmist said, *"he leadeth me beside the still waters"* (Psalms 23:2b). God wants to consistently lead you beside the still waters.

"Still waters" are waters that flow very slowly and calmly. They are shallow, quiet trickles of water gently flowing along. They aren't deep – ankle-high at most – the flow is slow, and the bubbling of the water is amazingly soothing. It's a place where you can breathe deeply and take in the sounds of nature.

This is the type of still waters David is talking about. In Hebrew, the words for 'still waters' in Psalms 23:2b means literally, "restful waters".

God wants to lead you to a place of rest, a place of trust, a place of confidence, a place where you rely on Him and focus on Him

Dr. Augusta Ogbene

without anything – any issues of life - distracting you. He wants to take the "heavy burdens" off your life and replace them with His everlasting peace and rest.

If you think a little deeper on Psalm 23, you'd realize that sheep are not able to swim and therefore, need a shepherd to guide them to waters that are still and safe for them. If one sheep fell into a fast flowing stream, with the heavy wool, death would be sudden.

To avoid any such calamity, the shepherd leads them to quiet, shallow waters where he knows they will be safe, if they will pay attention to him.

God knows the calamities that lie on the speed lane of life. Everyone wants to make it fast. Everyone wants to get established soon enough. Everyone wants to get what they want and on time too. But some of these things don't come in the easiest fashion.

Dr. Augusta Ogbene

In the process of running after the comforts and achievements of life, many get their fingers burnt.

To avoid the mishaps and dilemma that plague human life, the shepherd decides to take the lead, and guides you beside still waters – the way of peace and rest. He never leads you in the way of trouble. He knows just how to avoid the spots where you get in trouble. It is never His delight that you make mistakes that cost your peace.

Like any loving parent, it is not God's delight to see you consistently in regrets and tears. He builds you, stirs your nest to mature you, flutters over you and bears you on His wings, to keep you from the ways of sorrow, depression and pain.

This is why He said, "*I will **instruct thee** and **teach thee** in the way which thou shalt go: I will **guide thee** with mine eye*" (Psalms 32:8).

Dr. Augusta Ogbene

Notice the threefold repetition here: I will *instruct thee*, I will *teach thee*, I will *guide thee*. Instruct, teach and guide are three faces of the same process.

It is to show just how much God is interested in leading you safely, far above errors, costly mistakes and regrets. It goes a long way to explain how much He greatly desires that you have perfect peace in every step you take.

This was the very reason He purposed to lead Israel, but the people would not hearken to Him. At one time the Lord bared His mind to Moses and sympathized with the inability of Israel to take His instructions and be well guided.

He said to Moses in Deuteronomy 5:29, "*O that there were such an heart in them, that they would fear me, and keep all my commandments always, that it might be well with them, and with their children for ever!*"

Dr. Augusta Ogbene

If they listened to Him and kept His instructions, they would have walked in the way of peace and it would be well with them and their families. But they wouldn't.

Beloved, do you really desire to put an end to chaos in your life and experience peace? Follow God! Let Him guide you daily. Let His building, stirring, fluttering and bearing lead you to the place of surrendering totally to His leading, that it may be well with you.

Isaiah said of Him, "*Thou wilt keep him in perfect peace, whose mind is stayed on thee: because he trusteth in thee*" (Isaiah 26:3). Stay your mind on Him and let Him have the way!

He leadeth me, O blessed thought!
O words with heav'nly comfort fraught!
Whate'er I do, where'er I be
Still 'tis God's hand that leadeth me.

Dr. Augusta Ogbene

Refrain:
He leadeth me, He leadeth me,
By His own hand He leadeth me;
His faithful foll'wer I would be,
For by His hand He leadeth me."

Joseph H. Gilmore

AWAY FROM TEMPTATION

One of the reasons the Lord chooses to take the lead is to help us avoid or overcome temptation.

In the Lord's Prayer, the Lord Jesus told us to pray, *"Lead us not into temptation..."* (Matthew 6:13). Here, Jesus intended more than a prayer against our faith being tested for its authenticity. He had in mind situations that might pressure us to stumble and fall into sin.

Jesus was teaching us to pray that we may be protected when we find ourselves faced with

Dr. Augusta Ogbene

situations and enticements that would drag us away from loyalty to God.

Hear this: we sometimes have a desire for those things which are contrary to God's will. Often, it is only the lack of opportunity that keeps us from falling. When the desire and opportunity meet together, the moment can be very drastic.

When Jesus asked us to pray not to be led into temptation, He was asking us to pray that the Father, in His love and tenderness, will not allow any wrongful desire in our hearts meet the opportunity for its expression.

Think about it, has someone ever done something to you that made you feel like tearing them to pieces if you ever met them? But God never allowed your desire to meet with the opportunity.
Have you ever heard a story of how one

Dr. Augusta Ogbene

person was totally messed up by another, and you said to them, "If I were in your shoes, I would teach them a lesson they'd never forget."

But God never allowed you be in their shoes because He knows how weak you are, and what you're capable of doing. He would never allow your desire to meet with the opportunity.

God will always do everything in His mercy and power to lead you away from temptation. If He ever allowed you to come face-to-face with one, it is probable that He has already kept a great open door of escape.

The Bible says, "*There hath no temptation taken you but such as is common to man: but God is faithful, who will not suffer you to be tempted above that ye are able; but will with the temptation also make a way to escape, that ye may be able to bear it*" (1Corinthians 10:13).

Dr. Augusta Ogbene

This is why God is keen on leading you. He alone knows how to lead you away from temptation.

By shaking your nest as the eagle does, He trains you to mature out of certain dangerous things that could swallow your future. He knew that you were too raw to step into destiny. That was why He stirred your nest, to prune, saw, chisel, and sandpaper you for the future.

Without His stirring and fluttering, you would never develop the muscle to withstand the terribly stormy tests of the future.

This was where most of the Israelites failed. When God stirred their nests by bringing them into that lonely wilderness without water, it was time for them to mature in handling their bodily appetites. Rather than stoop to ask what God was up to, they spent more of their time complaining.

Dr. Augusta Ogbene

When the time came for them to withstand the seductions of the Moabitish girls fostered by Balaam and Balak, they failed.

Then again they fell headlong to their appetites and demanded for flesh to eat without appreciating what God had done for them. The Bible says that God *"gave them their request; but sent leanness into their soul"* (Psalms 106:15).

Only a few men among them who patiently trained to maturity in God's eagle school, were able to overcome the temptations that came their way.

Beloved, if God doesn't lead you, there will certainly be too many regrets in your life. There will be too many falling and rising, too many restitutions, and too many confessions of sin. His leading keeps you from being confronted with what can conquer you.

Dr. Augusta Ogbene

Have you been built, shaken, fluttered and borne on eagles' wings? Now let the Master lead you. Let the One Who's familiar with your weaknesses lead you away from temptations.

Give Him the chance to go ahead of you and prevent your unlawful desires from finding the opportunity for expression. He knows you; He knows where you're vulnerable, and He will lead you away from there. '*He leadeth me in the path of righteousness for His name's sake*" (Psalm 23:3).

My Lord knows the way through wilderness
All I have to do is follow
My Lord knows the way through the wilderness
All I have to do is follow
Strength for today is mine all the way
And all that I need for tomorrow
My Lord knows the way through the wilderness
All I have to do is follow

Dr. Augusta Ogbene

HE LEADS WITH THE EAGLE'S EYE

It is said that if a man swapped his eyes for an eagle's, he could see an ant crawling on the ground from the roof of a 10-storey building. Incredible, isn't it?

An eagle's eyeball is almost the same size as a human eye. Given that the eyeball is so large relative to the size of the head, an eagle's eyes fill most of the skull. Eagles use both monocular and binocular vision, meaning they can use their eyes independently or together depending on what they are looking at.

An eagle's eye has two focal points, one of which looks forward and the other to the side at about a 45 degrees angle. These two focal points, called foveae, allow eagles to see straight ahead and to the side simultaneously. An eagle can see something the size of a rabbit at more than three miles away.

Dr. Augusta Ogbene

Now, God doesn't have an eagle's eyesight but far more. The eagle sees in both directions – forward and sideward – but "*the eyes of the LORD run to and fro throughout the whole earth*" (2Chronicles 16:9). The eagle can see an object three miles away but the Lord looks down from heaven and sees everything going on in the earth.

Why does the Bible use the eagle to describe God's leading of His people? Simple: the eagle while soaring, can notice any movement in pretty much the entire broad area of earth below it. And of the Lord, Hebrews 4:13 says, "*Neither is there any creature that is not manifest in his sight: but all things are naked and opened unto the eyes of him with whom we have to do.*"

What this implies is that God can see far ahead of you. If I asked you what would happen in another two hours or two days from the time you are reading this book, you

Dr. Augusta Ogbene

would never be able to explain it. But God can. He can see vividly into a thousand years ahead. He knows every danger that lurks in the way and every success that awaits you.

The testimony was given of a young Christian girl in one of the universities in Nigeria. While travelling back to visit her parents, she boarded a bus and took a seat in front.

While on the seat, she heard a voice within her that said, "Change seat." She stood up from the front seat and went to the back seat of the vehicle. While sitting there she heard again, "Change seat." She got up and went to the middle part of the bus and sat there.

While they travelled along the way, a trailer failed brakes and ran into the bus from the front. Everyone that sat on the front seats, including the driver, died.

Dr. Augusta Ogbene

While that happened, another trailer ran into the bus from behind. Everyone on the back seats died. Only the people at the middle survived, though badly injured. But this girl came out unscathed.

The testimony is this: the God Who told her to change seats had already seen the calamity with those two trailers long before the journey started. He was the One Who went ahead of the young girl to lead her to safety, protect and preserve her, because He could see far into their journey.

Beloved you will never see calamity. You will never be an object of mishap or pity. The Lord shall lead you away from evil and bad news. He will deliver you from any wrong happening and keep you safe.
Where there's calamity of accident, fire outbreak, spiritual or physical attack, you shall never be found. The Lord will always see far ahead of you and deliver you from danger before time.

Dr. Augusta Ogbene

This is why God is very keen about leading you.

From the foregoing, I'm sure it has become very clear to you that there's a lot you can't see or know about. But God does. And because He knows all about tomorrow, He alone can lead you safely into it.

Get this: It is a complete lack of understanding to think that God does not know what you are going through in life. Tell me, would the eyes that see into the very end of your days on earth be so short-sighted that He cannot see what you go through at the moment? The Psalmist said, *"he that formed the eye, shall he not see?"* (Psalms 94:9)

God forbid! That is an aberration of thought. No matter what is happening in your life right now, like the sharpness of the eagle's focus, God sees everything clearly. And not just that He sees; He knows exactly

Dr. Augusta Ogbene

what He plans to do to bring you out of it with celebration and testimonies. Hallelujah!

All the Lord demands of you, is that you allow Him lead Him the way while you follow. Do not try to lead the way and then call on Him to come along. He wants to be in charge in every aspect of your life.

He wants to be in charge of your health: Call on Him before you call on the doctor. He wants to be in charge of your career: Speak to Him before you speak to an admissions officer. He wants to be in charge of your family: Tell Him about your marriage plans before you talk to your wife-to-be or husband-to-be.
The Lord sees far ahead, so only He can take you far ahead.

The Bible tells an interesting story in 2Chronicles 25 about a man called

Dr. Augusta Ogbene

Amaziah. He wanted to go to war and requested to get some extra hands to assist his army. The Bible says he *"paid $200,000 to hire 100,000 experienced mercenaries from Israel"* (2Chronicles 25:5, TLB).

200,000USD is quite a lot of money. But he never knew what was ahead of him. Nevertheless, because God was involved in his life, He chose to help him.

The Bible says in 2Chronicles 25:7, *"But there came a man of God to him, saying, O king, let not the army of Israel go with thee; for the LORD is not with Israel,.."*

When Amaziah paid to hire soldiers from Israel to assist him in war, he didn't know this. Of course, he couldn't see farther than where he was. But there was Someone Who could see far ahead into the battle – God! He knew that if Israel's hired soldiers joined Amaziah in that war, Amaziah would be defeated, so he warned the king ahead of time.

Dr. Augusta Ogbene

This is one reason why David always enquired of the Lord if he should go into battle or not. Whatever God told him was what he did, because he understood God's far sightedness. He knew that the Lord always saw the end of the battle before it began.

In 1Samuel 23:2 the Bible says, "*Therefore **David enquired of the LORD,** saying, Shall I go and smite these Philistines? **And the LORD said unto David, Go,** and smite the Philistines, and save Keilah.*"

In 1Samuel 23:4 the Bible says, "*Then **David enquired of the LORD** yet again. **And the LORD answered him and said, Arise, go** down to Keilah; for I will deliver the Philistines into thine hand.*"

In 2Samuel 2:1 the Bible says, "*And it came to pass after this, that **David enquired of the***

Dr. Augusta Ogbene

LORD, *saying, Shall I go up into any of the cities of Judah?* **And the LORD said unto him, Go up.** *And David said, Whither shall I go up? And he said, Unto Hebron."*

In 2Samuel 5:19 the Bible says, "*And* **David enquired of the LORD,** *saying, Shall I go up to the Philistines? wilt thou deliver them into mine hand?* **And the LORD said unto David, Go up:** *for I will doubtless deliver the Philistines into thine hand."*

However, in 2Samuel 5:23 the Bible says, "*And when* **David enquired of the LORD,** *he said,* **Thou shalt not go up;…"**

Like the case of King Amaziah, when God told David not to go up, it didn't mean that He was not powerful enough to give David victory, rather He was wise enough to save David unnecessary hassles and waste of time.

Dr. Augusta Ogbene

There are things the farsighted attribute of God, like the eagle, can save you from. If you can give God a chance to lead you, the sorrow, pain, depression and struggles of your present life can be handled.

If you can give Him a chance to lead you, the hassles of the future can be handled. There is nothing that will happen to you any time in the future that will take God by surprise. He always sees it before it ever happens.

The eagle can see only some miles away, but God sees thousands of years away.

All of God's building, breaking, fluttering, and bearing, is to mature you to give Him the chance to lead you with an eagle's focus, so you don't run into any danger ahead of you. But will you let Him?

Dr. Augusta Ogbene

HE LEADS YOU TO SUCCESS

One of the greatest longings of the human heart is to be successful. And one of the reasons God leads His own is to make them successful. He said in Isaiah 48:17b, "*I am the LORD thy God **which teacheth thee to profit**, which leadeth thee by the way that thou shouldest go.*"

Have you ever met one person who went into business with the idea of losing? I doubt that you have. Everyone attends college to be more useful in society and make a living through the application of what they studied.

Every person goes into business with the sole purpose of making profit and becoming successful. No one wants to go into anything of menial or no profit.

No one sets out to fail in life. It isn't our goal

Dr. Augusta Ogbene

to be last in line, unnoticed or forgotten. Instead, we are taught to market ourselves, go for the gold, develop our platform, and increase our following.

God understands the drive of the human heart. He understands how much you want to make it in life and enjoy peace and comfort. Yet He says to you, "I know the places where you can make the profit you want. I know the places where you can derive the comfort and peace you desire, and I can fix you there. You don't need any long leg to get there; My Leg is the longest you can ever see, and I can go ahead and make a way for you."

That is what God means when He says, "*I am the LORD thy God which teacheth thee to profit, which leadeth thee by the way that thou shouldest go.*" All He is saying is, "I am the only One that can lead you to "good success". Just give me a chance to lead you."

Dr. Augusta Ogbene

Beloved, God does not want you to die struggling. God does not want you to look like an escort for those who came on earth to be rich. No! You too were born to make a mark on the sands of time. But the only person that can lead you into that manifestation is God.

When He led Israel He said to them, "*I have given you **a land for which you did not labor**, and **cities which you did not build**, and you dwell in them; you eat of the **vineyards and olive groves which you did not plant**"* (Joshua 24:13, NKJV).

I'd like you to note the phrases in bold: "*a land for which you did not labour, cities which you did not build, and vineyards and olive groves which you did not plant.*" What that tells you is that God is able to give you "toil-less success."

If you are going to get everything by your

Dr. Augusta Ogbene

sweat, you could die before your time. Some things must come to you by the Mighty Hand of the Alpha and Omega.

The world – and your own intelligence – will tell you to work harder and strive more in order to make it, but God says, "*Be still and know that I am God*" (Psalm 46:10). In the King James Version, the phrase "Be still" is translated "Cease striving."

Beloved, if you would patiently submit under God's building, breaking, fluttering and bearing, He will surely make you to lie down in green pastures. Most people just want God to lead them to profiting in life, but they are not ready to pass through His painful pruning.

The process is painful because He wants to produce a people He can lead. And He cannot lead a people He has not processed.

Dr. Augusta Ogbene

Why do you think God left the roadway which would take the children of Israel just eleven days to get into Canaan, and rather passed them through a wilderness that took forty years? He needed to process them, so that He could lead them.

God is not deficient of prosperity. He has more than enough to make you successful and prosperous, but would you be led?

Psalms 4:6 says, *"Many, Lord, are asking, "Who will bring us prosperity?" Let the light of your face shine on us."* The light of His countenance is all you need to walk in super abundance.
But would you let Him shake your nest, flutter over you, and bear you on His wings, so that He might lead you?

So many children of God complain of suffering, but the big question is "Can you stand to be blessed?"

Dr. Augusta Ogbene

YOU MUST SURRENDER

Come live in me all my life, take over
Come breathe in me, I will rise on eagle's wings
Come live in me all my life, take over
Come breathe in me, I will rise on eagle's wings
Hillsong worship

Beloved, it's time to make the decision either to walk on your own or take the Master's Hand. It's time to make the decision either to strive for success on your own or let God lead you there.

It's time to make the decision to keep moving from one troubling issue to another or experience lasting peace from the Master's leading. It's time to decide whether to step into tomorrow naively or let God's eagle focus help you avoid the dangers ahead.

It's time to decide whether to willingly let

Dr. Augusta Ogbene

God into your boat (your marriage, project, or plans) so He can more quickly get you where He wants you to go or you want to try and get there on your own.

If your decision is to be led of the Master, there is the need for absolute surrender. To surrender to the Master is to admit that the life you live is not yours; it belongs to totally to Him. When you realize you were bought at a price (1Corinthians 6:20) and completely surrender all to Him, the life you find in return is the only one worth living.

If you have never really received Jesus Christ into your life, it is time to do so (please refer to back page of this book).

If you have been a Christian serving the Lord, it is time to surrender all and ask the Master to break you again and again and mould you into the person He has always desired to have as a vessel in His Hands.

Dr. Augusta Ogbene

Judson W. Van de Venter's hymn appeals so much to me at this moment. And I'm sure it will to you too:

All to Jesus I surrender,
All to Him I freely give;
I will ever love and trust Him,
In His presence daily live.

I surrender all,
I surrender all;
All to Thee, my blessed Savior,
I surrender all.

All to Jesus I surrender,
Humbly at His feet I bow;
Worldly pleasures all forsaken,
Take me, Jesus, take me now.

Beloved, God cares about who is in the driver's seat of your life — and He wants to be the One there. To have a heart that is completely His is to surrender and do things His way, right down to what you strive for and how you live day-to-day.

Dr. Augusta Ogbene

I invite you to surrender to God and serve Him out of love for Him, and not just because you want Him to bless you.

When you take the time to surrender completely to Him and let Him know that you are ready for anything He wants to do with your life, He brings a satisfaction to your soul, a joy to your heart, and productivity to your work that is both restful and successful.

Shalom!

Dr. Augusta Ogbene

PRAYER OF SALVATION

Beloved, if you have never asked the Lord Jesus to be your Lord and Saviour, I want to use this opportunity to ask you to do so. God operates by covenant. As you allow Jesus Christ into your life today, you enter a covenant with God where all His promises through Jesus are "yea and amen" in your life.

No man or woman can have access to God the Father except through His Son Jesus Christ. Please open up your heart and pray this prayer and mean it in your heart:

Dear Father, I come to you today (now) to confess all my sins in the past. I repent of all the sins now and ask for your Mercy and Forgiveness. I invite the Lord Jesus into my life to be my Lord and Savior. I renounce every link with satan and evil today. I confess with my mouth that Jesus is Lord! And I believe in my heart that God raised Him from the dead for my sake. Therefore I am saved. Thank you Heavenly Father for saving me. Please Lord, write my name in the Lamb's Book of Life. I pray in Jesus' Name. Amen! Thank you Father.

YES! You want your children to know the Lord and to walk in His ways. You want them to be useful in the hands of God, and to be a blessing to their generation.

■ You want your children to surpass your achievements in life. You want them to be exceptional, extraordinary, and outstanding. You want them to be history makers, world changers, trend setters and trail blazers.

■ You want your children to understand what God wants them to accomplish with their life on earth early enough.

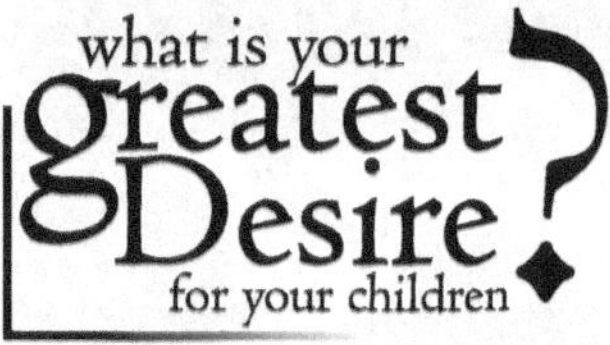

In this book, Dr. Augusta shares Word-proven practical steps to bringing out the hidden hero in your children. Now you have in your hands the tool to help your children fulfill God's unchanging purpose for their lives.

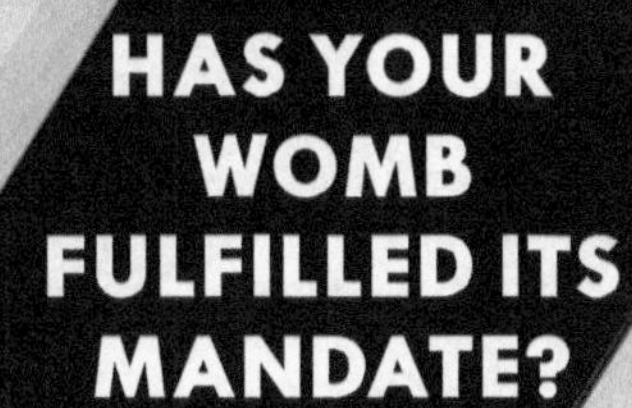

This book underscores the relevance, significance, and untapped power of the womb. It'll reshape every woman's thinking, remold her destiny and lead her to fulfill God's original mandate for her womb.

ETIQUETTE FOR THE CHRISTIAN WOMAN	GRACE MADE ROOM FOR ME	LIVE EXTRA-ORDINARY!	PRAYING FOR YOUR CHILDREN
Etiquette for the Christian Woman is an all round book specially designed for the all round building and rebuilding of the Christian woman. Dr Augusta here focuses on the beauty of the whole woman; beauty that works from the inside out. Written in a simple, straight forward and balanced style, the book takes care of the appearance, conduct, comportment, body care, character and lifestyle of the Christian woman at home and in public.	It is by God's grace that we find favour with God and man. Most of the time people don't even know why they like us, accept us, trust us, approve of us over others. They just do because God shines His light of grace upon us and gives us favour. Dr Augusta in this little impact full book, shares the story of grace in the life of Ruth. Nothing else but grace made room for her in a strange land. Nothing else but grace will make room for you in this life. Read this book, understand it, live it.	God releases His power according to the authority of His Word which you declare through prayers. Everything that can cause failure to man spiritually, physically, mentally, socially, or financially can get solved through the Book of Proverbs. A combination of the power of the Word and the power of prayer can transform any life, including yours. Praying through the Book of Proverbs will influence every aspect of your life and that of the people around you. Get ready to live extraordinary!	It is indeed, very difficult and dangerous to raise up children without adequate spiritual cover over them, especially that there is such overwhelming deluge of ungodliness in the rank and file of the society in which they grow. Until parents can learn to take their children to God on their knees, they may watch with dismay, the ungodly and strange habits the children may exhibit now and in their future lives. This book will help parents to resist in prayer, the spirit of this age from manifesting in the life of their children.